GROW YOUR MIND

WORK SMARTER

Written by Alice Harman
Illustrated by David Broadbent

CRABTREE
PUBLISHING COMPANY
WWW.CRABTREEBOOKS.COM

CRABTREE
PUBLISHING COMPANY
WWW.CRABTREEBOOKS.COM

Author: Alice Harman
Series designer: David Broadbent
Illustrator: David Broadbent
Editor: Crystal Sikkens
Proofreader: Melissa Boyce
Print coordinator: Katherine Berti

A trusted adult is a person (over 18 years old) in a child's life who makes them feel safe, comfortable, and supported. It might be a parent, teacher, family friend, social worker, or another adult.

Library and Archives Canada Cataloguing in Publication

Title: Work smarter / written by Alice Harman ; illustrated by David Broadbent.
Names: Harman, Alice, author. | Broadbent, David, 1977- illustrator.
Description: Series statement: Grow your mind | Includes index. |
 First published in Great Britain in 2020 by the Watts Publishing Group.
Identifiers: Canadiana (print) 20200222546 |
 Canadiana (ebook) 20200222775 |
 ISBN 9780778781721 (hardcover) |
 ISBN 9780778781806 (softcover) |
 ISBN 9781427125989 (HTML)
Subjects: LCSH: Success in children—Juvenile literature. | LCSH:
Self-actualization (Psychology) in children—Juvenile literature. |
 LCSH: Attention in children—Juvenile literature. | LCSH: Cognition in
children—Juvenile literature. | LCSH: Success—Juvenile literature. | LCSH:
 Self-actualization (Psychology)—Juvenile literature. | LCSH: Attention—
Juvenile literature. | LCSH: Thought and thinking—Juvenile literature.
Classification: LCC BF723.S77 H37 2021 | DDC j155.4/191—dc23

Library of Congress Cataloging-in-Publication Data

Names: Harman, Alice, author. | Broadbent, David, 1977- illustrator.
Title: Work smarter / written by Alice Harman ; illustrated by David
 Broadbent.
Description: New York, New York : Crabtree Publishing Company, 2021. |
 Series: Grow your mind | Includes index.
Identifiers: LCCN 2020015516 (print) |
 LCCN 2020015517 (ebook) |
 ISBN 9780778781721 (hardcover) |
 ISBN 9780778781806 (paperback) |
 ISBN 9781427125989 (ebook)
Subjects: LCSH: Behavior modification--Juvenile literature. |
 Habit breaking in children--Juvenile literature.
Classification: LCC BF637.B4 H355 2021 (print) | LCC BF637.B4 (ebook) |
 DDC 155.4/191--dc23
LC record available at https://lccn.loc.gov/2020015516
LC ebook record available at https://lccn.loc.gov/2020015517

Crabtree Publishing Company

www.crabtreebooks.com   1-800-387-7650
Published by Crabtree Publishing Company in 2021

Published in Canada
Crabtree Publishing
616 Welland Ave.
St. Catharines, Ontario
L2M 5V6

Published in the United States
Crabtree Publishing
347 Fifth Ave.
Suite 1402-145
New York, NY 10116

Printed in the U.S.A./082020/CG20200000

First published in Great Britain in 2020 by The Watts Publishing Group Copyright © The Watts Publishing Group 2020

CONTENTS

Mindsets at work

Have you ever gotten frustrated because you feel like you're working really, really hard but not actually making any progress?

It can be easy at these moments to fall into a **fixed mindset** way of thinking. This means believing that you can either do something or you can't, that you're either smart or not smart enough to understand something.

With this fixed mindset, it can feel like there's no point trying to challenge yourself and you might as well give up. But this just isn't true!

Our brains are always growing and changing. Everyone's brain has billions of **neurons**, which build bridges to pass information to each other. The things we do and think affect where these bridges are built and how strong they are.

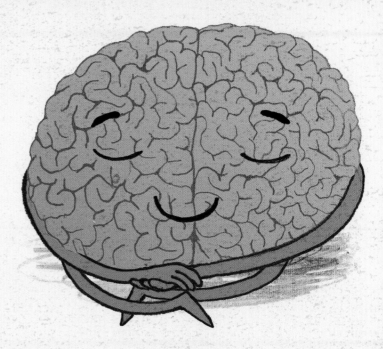

Understanding that you have the power to change your brain through your efforts is called a **growth mindset**. And developing a growth mindset is a great way to help you on your lifelong, brain-boosting journey.

Working hard and putting in a lot of effort, especially when things get difficult, is really important, but we can also learn how to work smarter. This means developing habits and systems to help make these efforts as effective as possible and keep our brains feeling calm and positive.

Let's get started!

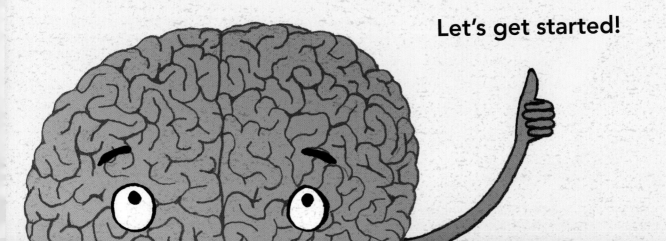

Fighting fit

We know we have to brush our teeth twice a day to keep them healthy and strong, but how do we take care of our brain?

Because the brain can do all kinds of amazing thinking, we can sometimes forget that it is a part of the body that also needs to be looked after properly.

No one's suggesting that you brush your brain (ew!), but there are a lot of other things you can do to keep it healthy and happy.

Sleeping well, eating healthy, exercising regularly, and drinking enough water all help us concentrate for longer, remember more information, and complete more challenging work.

In a notebook, start a picture diary to keep track of healthy habits that will help you work smarter. Every day, write down how many:

★ hours you slept the night before;

★ fruits and vegetables you've eaten;

★ glasses of water you've drunk;

★ half-hours of exercise you've done.

Add one of these faces to show how happy and focused you feel each day:

At the end of the week, add up the numbers for each day to get a total weekly score for sleep, healthy eating, water, and exercise. See if you can beat your score over the next week!

Look at the "feeling" faces that you've put for each day too. Can you see any patterns, such as feeling better if you've had more sleep the day before?

Get chunking!

Chunking means breaking down information or tasks into smaller chunks that are easier to work through one by one.

It can also make big tasks feel less scary. Rather than having to push and push yourself to reach your goal all at once, you have rest points along the way.

Chunking is a smarter way of working because it stops your brain from getting overloaded and feeling stressed. When this happens, it's harder to take in information and easier to fall into the fixed-mindset idea that you just can't do something.

Imagine you're trying to memorize a poem to say in class. Remembering it all at once is really hard, but if you start with just one line and build up from there, it's much easier.

Try chunking a piece of homework, a project, or a task that feels like quite a big challenge.

1.
With a trusted adult, think about how you can split up the work you need to do into smaller chunks, and what order they should go in.

2.
Try drawing the chunks on a piece of paper in a fun way—maybe they could be beads on a necklace string or puzzle pieces to fit together.

3.
The breaks between the chunks are very important. For each break, write down or draw something relaxing or fun you could do for a few minutes—maybe dance or read a page of your book.

4.
Decide how long each chunk should be and set a timer when you start each one. Check off the chunks as you go and celebrate when you've finished!

One thing at a time

Sometimes it can feel like we've been working at something forever, but have gotten nowhere. If we really think about it though, we were likely interrupting ourselves the whole time and not really giving our brains a chance to focus.

Scientists have found that our brains can't really **multitask**—that is, focus on more than one thing at a time. When we jump from one thing to another, it takes our brains a while to refocus each time, so it's not a smart way to work.

It can also mean it takes us a frustratingly long time to get things done, and we might feel like giving up altogether. Making an effort to build up your power of concentration can really maximize your work efforts in the long term.

Put on a timer as you start the first chunk (see pages 8–9) of a task or a piece of work. Keep a notebook close by.

Every time you get distracted from the task you want to focus on and start doing something else, bring yourself back and add a tally mark in the notebook.

Don't worry about giving yourself the tally marks, it doesn't mean you've "failed." The whole point of this activity is to train your brain, and that takes time!

Try to get a lower tally score for each chunk, and see if it helps you get more done in the same amount of time.

Activate your brain

Have you ever read a page of a book quickly and then not been able to remember anything about it afterward? Or listened to your teacher's instructions, but realized afterward that you didn't really take in what you were supposed to do?

You can learn a lot by reading, listening, and watching, but if you're not careful your brain can switch off!

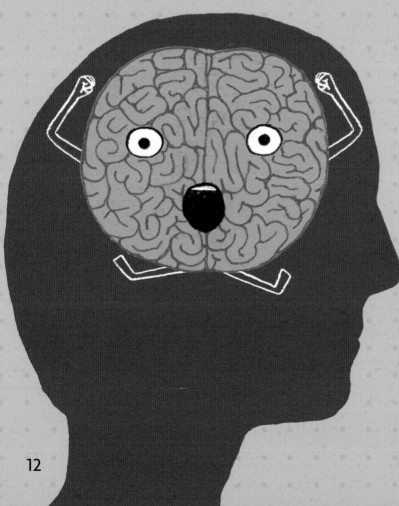

Work smarter by keeping your brain active when you're taking in information. For example, research shows that taking notes while listening and reading can help you remember information better.

Try asking questions before and during your lesson, either in your head or out loud. And try summing up what you've just learned in one sentence, as if you wanted to tell someone else.

Thea

A little while ago, I was getting really frustrated and upset because I couldn't remember things that I was just told in class or that I just read in a book.

I didn't want my teacher or my moms to think I wasn't trying, when I actually was. I didn't know what else to do.

We all talked about it after school one day, and my teacher suggested some ways I could be more active in my listening and reading. At home, I practiced asking questions and summing up the TV shows and books I watched and read, just for fun.

Now that I'm in the habit, it's easy! I remember things so much better and it's really helped me in class.

The next step

One of the best ways to work smarter is to understand what will challenge your brain without being so difficult that you feel frustrated and discouraged.

Picking the easiest option might feel safer than trying something challenging, but it won't be nearly as helpful in growing your brain.

If it's quite tricky, think about it as a longer-term goal. It might take a few steps to get there. You can feel really excited and proud that you're working hard toward it!

Rather than thinking of something as "too easy" or "too hard," try to think of it as the next step on your learning journey.

Try out these tips to help you pick a book that's just right for your next step—challenging but still enjoyable.

★ Think about what you want from the next book you read. Do you want to learn more about an interesting subject? Maybe you want to lose yourself in an exciting story? Look at a book's front cover and read the description on its back cover to decide whether it's what you're looking for.

★ Open a book to a double-page spread and try reading two pages. Can you read it very easily, understanding every word right away? If so, you might be ready for a more challenging book.

★ If you want to read a very challenging book with a lot of sentences you don't understand, ask an adult to read it with you. Take turns reading out loud, and talk about words you don't understand.

Give your brain a chance

If you are really struggling to understand something, it's important to ask an adult for help. Sometimes, we can be so frustrated with our brain not understanding something right away, we give up without giving it enough of a chance!

If you can't figure something out, try taking your time really looking at it again. Write down what you think it might be about, even if it feels like a guess, and what exactly you're finding confusing about it.

This is a great habit to develop because it makes it easier for others to help you. You might even find that something "clicks" during this process and you suddenly understand it better!

Sam

I've always found math difficult compared to my other classes. If I got stuck with my homework for even a second, I'd ask my parents for help.

My mom started encouraging me to read through the questions slowly a couple more times if I didn't understand them, thinking about what in particular I wanted to ask them about.

I discovered that a lot of the time I ended up understanding it better just by doing this, only wanting to check with my parents that I'd gotten it right.

Soon, I started feeling confident enough to do it by myself sometimes, and not worry if the answer wasn't right—it's all part of learning!

Keep repeating

Have you ever felt like you knew or understood something, but then it disappeared out of your brain or stopped making sense later on?

For our brains, learning something once is almost never enough. We need to go back over and over it, building up our knowledge until it really sticks.

Try making a schedule every time you learn something new. Go back to it the next day, then three days later, then a week later. Could someone quiz you between sessions?

Remember—repeating isn't a failure, it's a really smart way to work! Every time we make an effort to remember something, it helps us transfer the knowledge into our long-term memory.

Joel

I felt really embarrassed in science class because I just couldn't get the hang of things that everyone else seemed to understand.

I kept going back to the earlier sheets in my folder, looking at the answers I'd gotten wrong and still not really understanding why. I felt like I was never going to understand it properly or be able to figure out the correct answers by myself.

But, eventually, I did start remembering and understanding better, and I was really proud that I worked hard to grow my brain instead of giving up or pretending I understood.

Now I'm finding harder ideas easier to pick up because I know the basics inside out and upside down! And I feel confident that if I don't understand something, it's not forever. I just need to keep trying.

Nobody's perfect

Thinking in a "perfectionist" way means wanting everything you do to be perfect, and feeling really disappointed in yourself if you make a mistake.

Does that sound familiar? It does to a lot of people! It can be especially difficult not to think in this way if people tell us things such as "You're so smart" and "You're so good at that."

These comments seem nice, but they can actually make us worry so much about not living up to them that we don't want to take chances.

In reality, no one is perfect and we all make mistakes—and that's not a bad thing! Learning from mistakes is actually one of the most effective ways to grow your brain.

Over time, thinking positively about mistakes and viewing them as part of the learning process can strengthen the "I don't need to be perfect—I'm a learner!" bridges between neurons in your brain.

As these bridges get stronger than your "I must be perfect!" bridges, you'll find it gets easier to accept making mistakes, whether that's falling over in dance class or calling out a wrong answer at school.

Think of three positive statements you can repeat to yourself whenever you get worried about not doing something perfectly. For example, "I'm going to push myself to try something difficult and learn from the mistakes I make." Or, "I'm excited to see what I learn from the mistakes I make."

Write them down on a card you can keep in your pocket or backpack to look at and memorize. Happy brain training!

HOW DO THEY DO IT?

Even though we know that nobody's perfect, it can be hard sometimes not to compare ourselves to others. We might feel bad if we think they're doing "better" than us and seem to find it much easier.

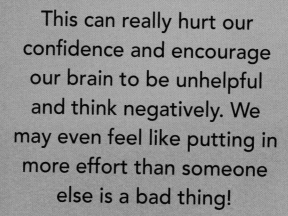

This can really hurt our confidence and encourage our brain to be unhelpful and think negatively. We may even feel like putting in more effort than someone else is a bad thing!

A smarter way to work is to learn to take lessons where you can from how people are working, rather than focusing on the results. Remember that you're on your own learning journey and what works for them may not work for you, but it's worth trying!

Poppy

I used to not like sitting next to Yolande because she always knew the right answers and remembered everything. It made me feel really bad about myself.

I complained to my foster dad one evening and he helped me see things a bit differently. He encouraged me to focus on what I could learn from Yolande's efforts rather than comparing our results.

We practiced changing thoughts like "It's so unfair, she's so smart!" to positive ones like "I can see that she asks questions in class and makes neat notes so she can read back over them."

Now I'm trying some of Yolande's good habits and they're working well for me too. I feel much more confident—and I thanked her for inspiring me!

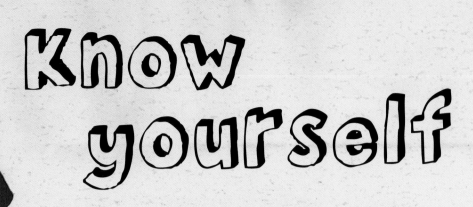

Know yourself

We can work smarter by understanding what we find easier and harder, and the different approaches we might need to develop and practice in each case.

With things we find easier, it can be tempting to think, "I'm good at that" in a fixed-mindset way. This can mean we don't try as hard at them, and may feel worried or upset when they start to feel more challenging.

With things that we find more difficult, on the other hand, we might think, "Oh, I'm not good at that" and try to avoid them or use this fixed-mindset judgment as an excuse not to try.

With an adult, draw an "Easyometer" on a large piece of paper, with a scale from 1–10. (1 = very hard and 10 = very easy.)

Write down different subjects, hobbies, and tasks on mini sticky notes and give them a 1–10 score of how easy you find them at the moment. Stick the notes in the right place on your Easyometer.

Make a plan for the next week, trying to alternate things you find easier and harder.

Every week, look at your Easyometer and move the sticky notes if you feel things have gotten easier or harder. You can see your learning journey in action!

1

2

3

4

5

6

7

8

9

10

WORK SMART, PLAY SMART

Our brain doesn't just learn when we sit down and study—it's always growing and changing.

When we're playing and having fun, we can still develop new skills and take in all kinds of information from the world around us. Just as we can learn how to work smarter, we can also discover ways to play smarter!

One of the best ways to play smarter is to try out a wide range of new activities and experiences that challenge us in different ways. Using our imagination to come up with new games, make up songs, put on shows, and more can also be a great way to boost our brainpower while having fun!

Make a list of 10 fun things you'd like to try doing on the weekend or in the evenings. It can be anything from ice skating to making your own treasure hunt!

Leave some space under each fun idea to draw or write about it once you've given it a try. How did it make you feel? Did you like it? What do you think you learned from it?

When you've tried everything on the list, make a new one! Keep the old lists for ideas. For example, if you enjoyed making up a song, how about recording it and then making up a dance routine?

You're the teacher

A great way to learn more effectively is to explain things to others and help them learn too. You can be a student and a teacher at the same time!

Helping another person do or understand something helps you think really clearly and carefully about it. By doing this, you end up learning more and feeling more confident. It can also strengthen the neuron-connecting bridges in your brain, helping you to remember information more easily. Nice!

In the evening, try teaching your parents or guardians what you learned at school that day—they might pick up a thing or two from you...

Robin

I like drawing and painting a lot, but I never thought I was very good at it. One day at school, we started a class project where we all drew and painted different zoo animals to stick together into a big scene on the wall. Fun!

After a while, though, I noticed that Maisie—the girl next to me—had stopped drawing and looked upset. I asked her what was wrong and she told me she was trying to draw a zebra but she couldn't make it look right.

I'd read a book about drawing animals and I remembered a bit about how to draw a horse, which looks a lot like a zebra. So I showed her what I learned about using circles and lines to get the shape right.

She tried really hard to do what I taught her and was much happier with how it looked. I felt good about that and it helped me feel more confident about my drawing too!

KEEP WORKING SMARTER!

Read through this book's smart-working tips any time you need a quick reminder!

Keep your brain healthy by sleeping well, eating nutritious, or healthy, foods, exercising regularly, and drinking plenty of water.

Break information or tasks down into smaller chunks and take breaks between them.

Stop trying to do a lot of things at once. Give your brain a chance to focus on one thing at a time.

Keep your brain active by taking notes and asking questions while you're listening and reading.

Figure out what the right next step is for you. It should be a bit of a challenge, but not so big that you get frustrated.

Ask for help when you need it, but try giving your brain a chance to figure things out first.

Repeat things you've recently learned over and over, to help them really stick in your brain.

Remember that no one is perfect, and you can learn a lot from making mistakes.

Instead of comparing yourself to others, think about how you can learn useful lessons from them for your own learning journey.

Create an Easyometer to track what you find easy and more difficult, and how your learning journey is progressing.

Play smart by coming up with all kinds of new games and imaginative ideas for having fun.

Turn yourself into a teacher, and boost your learning by explaining things to other people.

Glossary

chunking   Breaking down information or tasks into smaller chunks that are easier to work through one by one

fixed mindset   If you are using a fixed mindset, you believe that your intelligence is fixed and can't be changed

growth mindset   If you are using a growth mindset, you believe that your intelligence is always changing because your brain can grow stronger

multitask   To try to focus on more than one thing at once

neurons   Cells in your brain that pass information back and forth to each other

Index

Notes for adults

The concept of a "growth mindset" was developed by psychologist Carol Dweck, and is used to describe a way in which effective learners view themselves as being on a constant journey to develop their intelligence. This is supported by studies showing how our brains continue to develop throughout our lives, rather than intelligence and ability being static.

Responding with a growth mindset means being eager to learn more and seeing that making mistakes and getting feedback about how to improve are important parts of that journey.

A growth mindset is at one end of a continuum, and learners move between this and a "fixed mindset"—which is based on the belief that you're either smart or you're not.

A fixed mindset is unhelpful because it can make learners feel they need to "prove" rather than develop their intelligence. They may avoid challenges, not wanting to risk failing at anything, and this reluctance to make mistakes—and learn from them—can negatively affect the learning process.

Help children develop a growth mindset by:

- Giving specific positive feedback on their learning efforts, such as "Well done, you've been practicing…" rather than non-specific praise, such as "Good effort" or comments such as "Smart girl/boy!" that can encourage fixed-mindset thinking.

- Sharing times when you have had to persevere learning something new and what helped you succeed.

- Encouraging them to keep a learning journal, where they can explore what they learn from new challenges and experiences.

- Setting a regular time every day to check how things are going for them, and if they are feeling frustrated or stuck, talking over different ideas that can help them boost their efforts.